LINE, BAR, AND CIRCLE GRAPHS

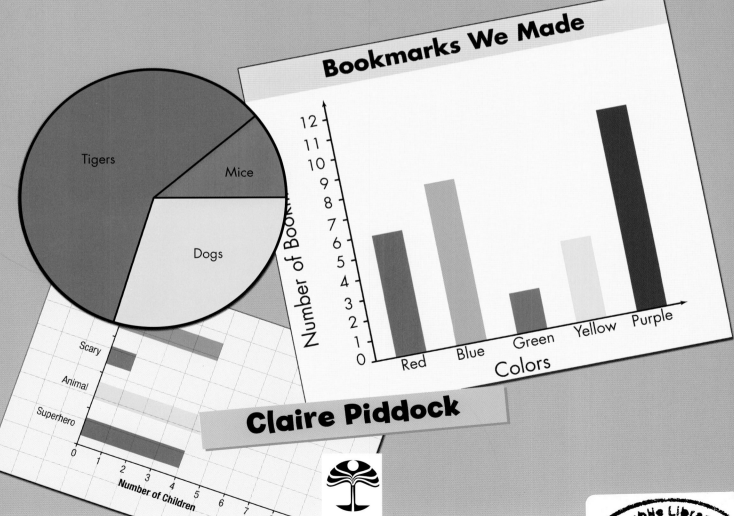

Claire Piddock

Crabtree Publishing Company
www.crabtreebooks.com

Author: Claire Piddock
Publishing plan research and development:
 Sean Charlebois, Reagan Miller
 Crabtree Publishing Company
Editor: Molly Aloian
Editorial director: Kathy Middleton
Project coordinator: Margaret Salter
Prepress technician: Margaret Salter
Coordinating editor: Chester Fisher
Series editor: Jessica Cohn
Project manager: Kumar Kunal (Q2AMEDIA)
Art direction: Rahul Dhiman (Q2AMEDIA)
Cover design: Shruti Aggarwal (Q2AMEDIA)
Design: Cheena Yadav, Supriya Manna (Q2AMEDIA)
Photo research: Debarata Sen (Q2AMEDIA)

Photographs:
Dreamstime: Jiang Daohua: p. 9 (bottom right)
Istockphoto: p. 9 (middle); Ron: p. 19
Photostogo: p. 5
Photolibrary: Sylvian Grandadam: p. 9 (top); Leah Warkentin:
 p. 13, 23; Jean-Paul Nacivet: p. 15
Q2A Media Art Bank: title page, p. 4, 6, 7, 8, 10, 11, 12, 15, 16, 18, 21
Shutterstock: Iofoto: front cover; Kot: p. 9 (bottom left); Parfta:
 p. 11 (middle); Gelpi: p. 11 (bottom left); Pamela Uyttendaele:
 p. 11 (bottom right); Christian Musat: p. 17 (top); Jirsak: p. 17
 (top left); Eric Isselée: p. 17 (top right and middle); Utekhina
 Anna: p. 17 (middle); Victor Soares: p. 17 (bottom left); Bill
 Kennedy: p. 17 (bottom right)

Library and Archives Canada Cataloguing in Publication

Piddock, Claire
 Line, bar and circle graphs / Claire Piddock.

(My path to math)
Includes index.
ISBN 978-0-7787-5247-9 (bound).--ISBN 978-0-7787-5294-3 (pbk.)

 1. Graphic methods--Juvenile literature. 2. Mathematics--Charts,
diagrams, etc.--Juvenile literature. I. Title. II. Series: My path to math

QA90.P53 2009   j518'.23   C2009-905366-7

Library of Congress Cataloging-in-Publication Data

Piddock, Claire.
 Line, Bar, and Circle graphs / Claire Piddock.
  p. cm. -- (My path to math)
 Includes index.
 ISBN 978-0-7787-5247-9 (reinforced lib. bdg. : alk. paper) -- ISBN 978-0-7787-
5294-3 (pbk. : alk. paper)
 1. Graphic methods--Juvenile literature. 2. Mathematics--Charts, diagrams, etc.-
-Juvenile literature. I. Title. II. Series.

 QA90.P476 2010
 511'.5--dc22
                                        2009035495

Crabtree Publishing Company

www.crabtreebooks.com   1-800-387-7650

Printed in China/122009/CT20090903

Published in Canada
Crabtree Publishing
616 Welland Ave.
St. Catharines, ON
L2M 5V6

Published in the United States
Crabtree Publishing
PMB 59051
350 Fifth Avenue, 59th Floor
New York, New York 10118

Published in the United Kingdom
Crabtree Publishing
Maritime House
Basin Road North, Hove
BN41 1WR

Published in Australia
Crabtree Publishing
386 Mt. Alexander Rd.
Ascot Vale (Melbourne)
VIC 3032

Contents

Summer Reading

The library has a summer reading club. The children who join soon find out that Lily, the librarian, loves using charts and graphs! First, she shows them a chart with their names.

Girls:	Michelle	Rachel	Jasmine	Briana	Elaine	Kate	Alicia	Carmen

Boys:	Steven	Max	Will	John	Dave	Duane

Then Lily makes a **pictograph** with the same information.

A pictograph is a shortcut way to show information. A pictograph has pictures and a **key**. The key tells you what each picture means. In this pictograph, one ☺ stands for "two children."

Activity Box

 means "two children." What does mean?

Michelle joins the club every summer.

Bar Graph

Lily asks the children what kinds of books they like. The information that Lily gathers is **data**.

Favorite Kinds of Books		
Books	**Tally**	**Number**
Funny	||||	4
Scary	|	1
Animal	|||||	5
Superhero	||||	4

This row shows that four children like funny books.

The marks in this column are tallies.

This column shows the total number of tallies counted.

She puts the data on a chart, using marks called tallies. The new chart is called a **tally chart**.

Activity Box

Look at the bar graph on the next page. Which kind of book is the least favorite?

Favorite Kinds of Books

The title tells what the graph is about.

Kinds of Books

Funny

Scary

Animal

Superhero

0 1 2 3 4 5 6 7 8 9 10

Number of Children

This scale goes from 0 to 10.

Lily then makes a **bar graph** to show the data another way. The numbers on the bottom of the graph are called a **scale**. The bars lie sideways. The ends of the bars show the number of each kind of book. You can read the scale to see the number each bar shows.

More Bar Graphs

Lily helps the children find the books they want to read. She gives them ideas for other kinds of books, too. She places books about countries, sports, and people on a table.

This bar graph shows the number of each kind of book. The bars of this graph stand straight up. The tops of the bars show the number of each kind of book on the table.

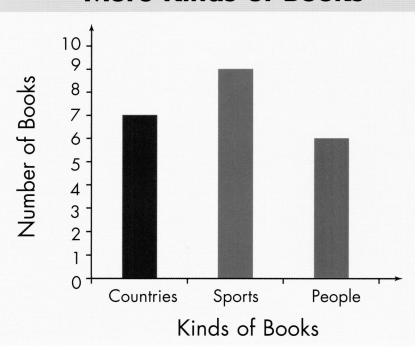

More Kinds of Books

Activity Box

How many sports books are on the table?
How many books about people are there?

Steven chooses a book about Canada. What kind of book would you choose?

What Graphs Say

You can get a lot of information from graphs. Graphs help people compare data. The children in the reading program made bookmarks. This bar graph shows the colors of the bookmarks the children made.

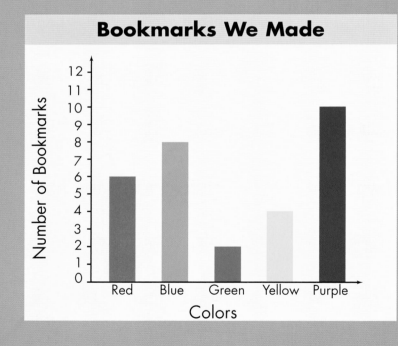

The graph shows that the color that was used the least was green. Subtract to find out how many more purple bookmarks were made than green.

10 - 2 = 8

Activity Box

How many bookmarks did the children make altogether? Add all of the numbers to find out.

The bookmarks were counted
and shown on the graph.

Line Graph

Lily reads a story during story time at the library. She keeps track of the number of children who stay for story time each day. She makes a **line graph** to show her data. A line graph is the best way to show how data changes over time.

A line graph also has a scale of numbers.

The points tell the number of children. The lines show the changes from day to day.

There were nine children on Monday. There were six on Tuesday.

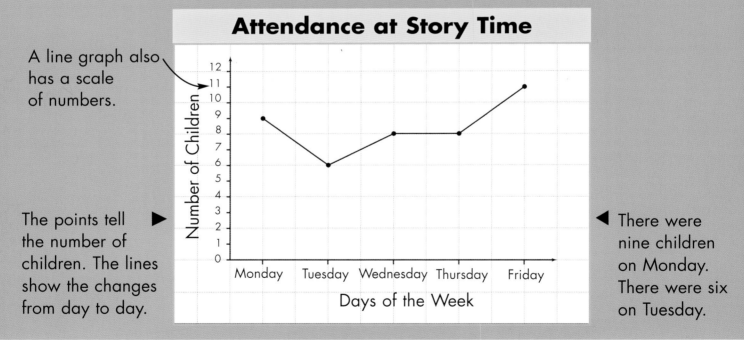

Attendance at Story Time

Number of Children vs. *Days of the Week*

Activity Box

Look at the line graph. On which day did the most children come for story time? Which two days had the same attendance?

Attendance is a record
of the number of people.

More Line Graphs

Max and his family go camping for a week. He keeps track of the time he spends reading books for the summer book club.

Max makes a line graph showing the number of minutes he spends each day on reading. The highest point on the graph is at 30 minutes. The highest point is called the **maximum number**. The lowest point is at five minutes. The lowest point is called the **minimum number**.

After his vacation, Max shows Lily and the other children his graph. "Why did you spend only five minutes reading on Tuesday, Max?" asks Lily. The other children know why. They all laugh and say, "Max was having too much fun at the beach!"

Activity Box

Did Max read the same amount every day? Which days did he read the most? Which day did he read for 10 minutes?

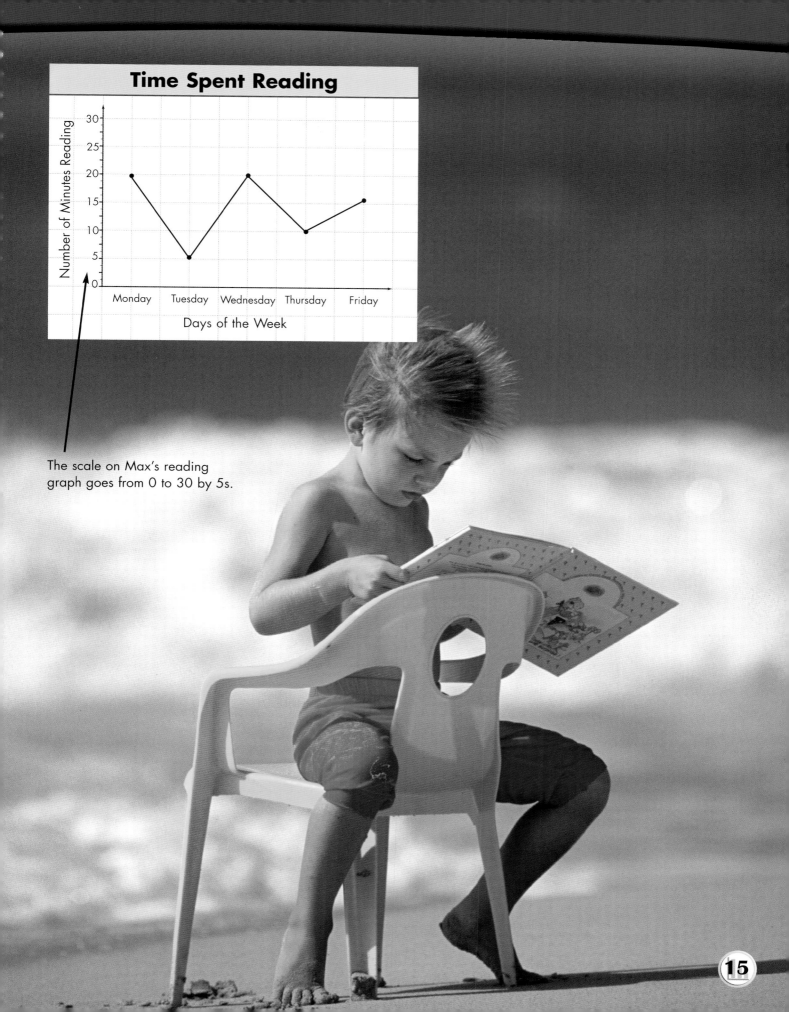

Time Spent Reading

The scale on Max's reading graph goes from 0 to 30 by 5s.

Circle Graph

The club members read both fiction and nonfiction books. Fiction is a made-up story. Nonfiction books are about true events.

Lily makes a **circle graph** that shows how much fiction and nonfiction they read. A circle graph shows a whole circle divided into parts. She makes a second circle graph about the kinds of animal stories they read.

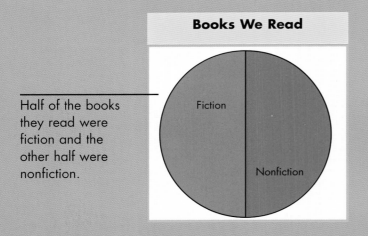

Books We Read

Fiction

Nonfiction

Half of the books they read were fiction and the other half were nonfiction.

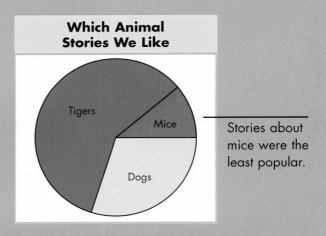

Which Animal Stories We Like

Tigers

Mice

Dogs

Stories about mice were the least popular.

Activity Box

Look at the circle graph with three parts. The parts are not equal. Do more children like books about dogs or books about tigers?

Which of these books would you like to read?

Line Plot

When the summer is over, Lily makes a list of all the children and how many books each child read.

Alicia 7	Briana 7	Carmen 5	Dave 6	Duane 6	Elaine 4	Jasmine 6
John 5	Kate 3	Max 3	Michelle 8	Rachel 7	Steven 5	Will 6

Lily then makes a **line plot** of this data. A line plot shows data on a number line. Lily makes one X above each number on the number line for each child who read that number of books.

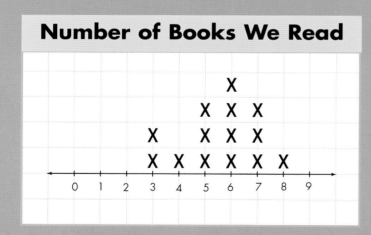

◀ There are 14 children, so there are 14 marks in total.

Activity Box

How many children read six books? What is the greatest number of books that one child read?

Kate read three books. On the line plot, her X is above the 3.

Many Books, Many Graphs

The children in the summer reading club had loads of fun with Lily, the librarian. They heard stories, made bookmarks, and read many, many books.

They learned different ways to show data in graphs. Can you match these questions to the correct graphs on the next page?

1. Which graphs show parts of a whole circle?

2. Which graphs show data changing over time?

3. Which graph uses an X to mean one child?

4. Which graphs help compare data?

Attendance at Story Time

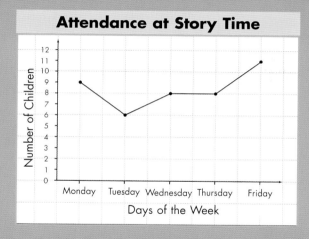

Time Spent Reading

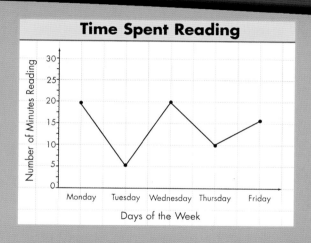

Favorite Kinds of Books

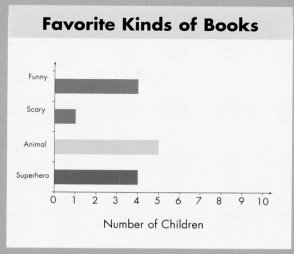

Bookmarks We Made

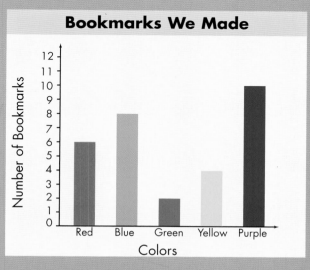

More Kinds of Books

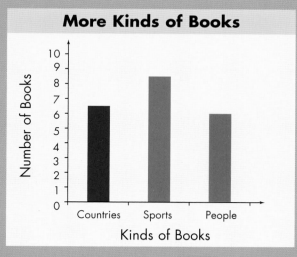

Number of Books We Read

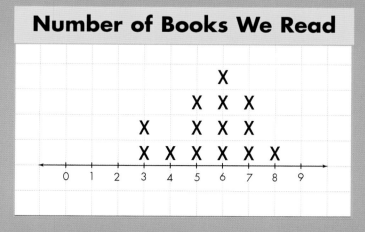

Books We Read

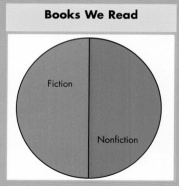

Which Animal Stories We Like

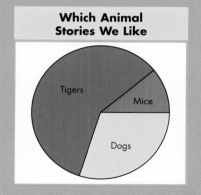

Glossary

bar graph Graph that uses rectangles that look like bars to show number information

circle graph Graph that shows data as a whole circle made up of different parts

data Information that is collected about people or things

key A set of small pictures in which each picture can stand for one or more pieces of data

line graph Graph that uses lines to show how data changes over time

line plot Diagram that shows data on a number line

maximum number The greatest (highest) number in a set of data

minimum number The least (lowest) number in a set of data

pictograph Data shown with pictures and a key

scale Numbers on a graph that help you read what the graph shows

tally chart A chart that uses lines in a row (tally marks) to record data

Index